from
Marsha Wood
Christmas 1978

CAROL CLARK OTTESEN

BOOKCRAFT INC.
SALT LAKE CITY, UTAH

Library of Congress Catalog Card Number: 75-4327
ISBN 0-88494-279-1

2nd Printing, 1978

LITHOGRAPHED IN U.S.A. BY
PUBLISHERS PRESS
SALT LAKE CITY, UTAH

CONTENTS

SOME PEOPLE DIE

Some people die
before they're dead.
In homemade coffins,
eaten alive by regrets
for songs not sung,
seas not sailed,
love not earned
or given,
they make a hell
waiting for heaven.

1

MARY'S APRIL IN BETHLEHEM

Mary,
Child-wife of innocence,
For Joseph, with sweet restraint
Has known her not.
Yet she,
Divinely overshadowed
Is filled with the seed of God.

Bear now the pain,
Forgotten by tomorrow.
All the strife
Has proven a small price
To pay for life.

A small cry
Pierces all the darkness
Of the world,
The mother holds Him close:

"O, you are so *small!*
Not more than just
A fold of swaddling cloth
With glory dancing
'Round your head.
(That squirming makes you red!)
Ah, mortality is hunger.
Have me.
Have me,
While there's starshine
On your heels
And moonbeams trailing
From your shoulders,
Let me feel your song
                    of somewhere else!

2

For I could
Shout with angels
Not just for your divinity,
But for the joy that says
You're part of *me!*
Behold, thy handmaid, Lord,
And though I nearly burst
With news of God on earth
                and of my part,
I know I must keep
                this rare secret
                        in my heart!"

3

SOLITARY CONFINEMENT

There's a time

For turning inside out

And sitting face to face

      with your lining,

Airing out stuffiness,

Repairing frayed

      thread ends,

        finding

Hours for dialogue

And deep soul bends,

      binding

In with out,

Listening

    for voices of your own,

A time for knowing some things

      must be done alone.

4

UPON FINDING YOU LOVE ME

Something goes singing

On a wind-spun arrow flying

For some celestial mark,

Beyond the eye-response,

The body-boundaries,

Too confining

For the something singing,

Singing,

Singing,

In my heart!

5

THE KISS

We brush like velvet cattails

in the wind

and rise like restless mallards

on the marsh,

first one, then two

until

five hundred fluttering wings

in one immense polyphony of sound

block out the world

then

settle

like a feather on a leaf,

quaking and quivering

with joy.

6

WAITING FOR YOU

I tidy my mind's room for you,
Polishing my wit,
Dusting a place
For you to sit,
A choice place
Brightly lit.

You come!
The vastness of your presence
Fills my room,
Splitting me to pieces
With your thrust of light!
O words are weak
Against this great synaptic power,
For with one thought, one touch
We gather like the chroma
Of a huge kaleidoscope
Into a grand design
That pierces Heaven
And lets us hold the stars!

ON LOOKING IN THE MIRROR

Mirror image,

Mere image.

The mirror imitates.

I'd rather look through

A window

For a wider, clearer view.

People, too.

I've known lots of mirrors,

But windows, far too few.

8

IF YOU WOULD BE A FRIEND

Don't tiptoe around my feelings
As if they'd wake up screaming —

But come firmly
With truth, as you see,
To sound against
My reality,
For friendship walks,
If it be true,
With a grain of resistance
In its shoe.

9

ANOTHER MARTHA

Martha's sitting on a box

With her soul in it.

Sometimes she lifts the corner

To let it breathe,

Then pinches off its nose

To hurry back to schedule.

Once her husband nearly

Unhinged the lid

But Martha quickly snapped it back

Before too much exposure

Would make it grow

And get in the way

Of cleaning house.

Martha's sitting on an empty box.

10

P.G.

My clothing shrinks now every week,
It won't last the duration.
The steering wheel sticks out too far,
I frequent every station.

11

But yet there's something quite profound
About this situation.
No more a single enterprise,
I'm a full-fledged corporation!

THOUGHTS ON LABOR DAY

The very best bargain

(Which is putting it mild)

Is ten hours labor

For a custom-made child.

12

HEY!

If I came to the earth

To watch and sit,

I'd be wasting the cherry

And eating the pit.

THE FLAME OF KNOWLEDGE

We hear today

From PTA

And other clubs-go-rightly,

To take our kids,

Light up their lids,

Fire up their searching brightly.

13

Now I've cajoled,

Kindled and told,

Sparked, fanned and rushed 'em.

I'm weary now

And hoping for

Spontaneous combustion!

DAY AT THE BEACH

I want to freeze these waves

And make this hour expand

While you are small

And malleable as sand.

See

Sand in my hands

Cupped full,

One I tightly press,

Soon every grain

Is gone.

The other I keep open

And my hand stays full.

I plan for you,

My son,

The second hand.

It is by force

We lose the sand.

14

FIRST DEER HUNT

Fire-colored leaves
Begin to crackle
Late October
That it's time —
Buck fever!
Gun-oil-spicy,
Knives spit-polished,
Bullets tamped,
Red . . . on red,
Thoughts of glory
For being just sixteen
And worthy of a gun.
But on that morning
When the sun lit up
Yellow aspens into gold
And sprinkled diamonds
On the snow at timberline,
He sat there on the mountain
                    hoping
        no one would come and see
        his gun lying against a tree.

15

LEAVING

I'm wondering now
why you are six-two
and I'm five-four
and your mother.
You stand all golden,
shower-wet tendrils curling
'round your ears,
ruddy-shiny seventeen
with feet that don't fit —
feet that kicked my womb
a yesterday ago
kick again
and you must go
while I feel traces
of the same old pain.

16

TO MY YOUNG SON DYING OF LEUKEMIA

I needed to come here,
Just with you,
Far to this misty ocean place
Of sea and blue
To feel the pulse of God.
But you came
To find a clump
Of limp seaweed
To take me by surprise
Or watch a sea hare
Left by the sea's rise
Purple with fright,
Raging hard
Against the night
And sure death on the rocks.

I tried to hold you
But you wriggled free . . .
Challenged, you run
Just like the sea
Catching the sun.
Waves tumble before
Sea tongues lick your toes,
Their rhythm pounding out
Eternal verse.
They call to you,
"Soon you must move
With the constant beat
Of the universe."

So I'll wait here,
Holding my dreams in empty arms,
Now folding them away
To dream no doubt
Another day.

TEACHER'S LAMENT THE SECOND WEEK OF SCHOOL

18

They come naked of love

And clothed with money.

Most mothers can give milk

But so few honey.

TEACHER TO STUDENT

I could give you

All my cut flowers,

        But there's a chance

You'd never learn

The thrill of growing

        Your own plants.

19

CHARITY FAILETH

20

He dropped a dime

In the cup of the blind,

Paid money to causes

Of every kind,

Gave hours of time

To those in despair

And locked his son out

'Til he cut his hair.

BEN YAZZI'S FIRST DAY

My sons,

Grown in hothouse soil,

Said why did Ben hide

A paring knife

In his sock

The first day

In white man's school?

It's generations of mistrust,

I said.

He grew like a briar

In shadows of the past.

We hold his hand

Until

His thorns drop off.

21

TO MY INDIAN SON LEAVING FOR THE RESERVATION

Child of Shadow Mountain,
Coyote brother of the desert,
Son.
Go now.
Slip your brown hand away,
A black-haired mother waits.

Bareback you rode
Into our saddled lives.
How far from here to there?
A white skin and
A century away.
Somehow we bridged the gap.

But I was not prepared
For this tearing I feel.
We wove you in the fabric
Of our life.
Our pattern will be rent
Till you return.

22

CONTEMPLATION WHILE SITTING ON A CORN CHIP

Something's got to give.

We don't live

Sterile

Like a Lysol-ed tub,

Antiseptic (there's the rub!)

. . . No germination

Of any kind . . .

So if I find

A corn chip on my chair

It may stay there

With several fingermarks and such

(I won't complain too much)

As long as home is fertile ground

For sprouting thoughts,

Where seedlings rise and dare

And kept with plan enough

To show I care.

23

QUIXOTIC

Mothers tell us such sweet lies.

"You're wonderful, you are!"

She couldn't possibly believe that,

Yet she robed me

In such elegant conceit

I spend my life

      Matching my shadow.

24

PINK CHERRY TREES AND WHITE LIES

From far away they looked like
Sticks of cotton candy, pink,
Framing the oval mirror called Potomac,
These tissue-blossomed cherry trees
They wished to tear out in the wartime
For they were Japanese.

Their beauty took my breath
And pulled me close enough to kiss.
I marveled at the heavenly craft,
Touched noses with a fragile blossom
Wishing hard to take just one
To deepen pleasure with possession.

A child would be suspected,
Especially if she were only eight.
Don't touch — the law, you know.
But there upon the ground
A perfect, fallen cluster called
"Pick me up" — I looked around.

No — in my hand
Who could ever tell?
I wouldn't be believed
But for the worst.
So I gently picked it up and
Hid it in my purse.

TO ONE ASKING FOR COUNSEL

26

Ask me not to judge for you —
Only widen your dimension,
For truth is its own advocate
And needs no intervention.

CHANGE

There's nowhere to hide;

Not under a prayer

Or well-paid tithe,

Nor behind the shoulders

Of the wise,

      Nor under the bed . . .

      Or being dead.

Bushels of good are never enough

To cover the edge of wrong,

      So accept my naked song

      of change, O God.

There's nowhere to hide.

FUGUE

I can't tell today

Where fingers end

      And keys begin.

This organ amplifies

My unarticulated

      hymn.

28

So would I find keys

To God's rhythm

      and intent,

That with one firm touch

I might be

      His instrument.

PROGRESS

Paper napkins

Paper dolls,

Plastic flowers,

Plastic balls,

Disposable spoons,

Throw-away knives,

Disposable husbands,

Throw-away wives,

Cardboard chairs

And building facades,

Plastic people,

Dispensable Gods.

29

BODY LANGUAGE

I wondered at the opulence

Of man-made temples,

The vanity of flowers,

Tediously tended,

Until I marvelled

At the excellence

Of God's temple

Made to house

Our spirits.

How watchfully

It must be tended,

Weeded, flowered,

Acknowledged

As equal part

To spirit

Or the fullness

Of our joy

Will never bloom.

TOUCHING

A back rub by mother

Was luxury,

So together it was,

Like you searching for me

Gently in the night,

Folding me close.

And

Just as real is

Reaching out for God,

Feeling the surge

Of lifting up!

Spiritual

Is

So

Physical.

31

BECOMING

If there is a stepping out of this skin
to see the world
and worlds,

if staying-alive cares
do not eclipse
the light of truth,

if our micro-view
shows a spot
of eternal becoming
then,
only then,
we live.

32

GENESIS

I wonder how God felt

When He first saw me.

Did He hold me lovingly

As fathers do,

Gingerly counting toes,

Checking flaws?

Perhaps He did

For now He knows

My need precisely.

    His spirit, warm and measureless,

    Is mine genetically

    And whispers, child,

    I want you back with me.

33

ARRIVAL IN TAIPEI

Beggar at the bus window,

Legs bowed with rickets,

Go away

And let me go

Around the world

Without touching it.

My coin is but a half-

Grain of sand

In poverty's flat purse.

Yes, leave.

Then I can wonder why

You are there

And I am here

And let my body retch

For a world

I didn't know was there.

34

HANDICAPPED

Hurrah

For the three-legged dog

Jogging the street

And the deaf white cat

Avoiding cars.

Only humans

Know they're defective

And let maggots

Chew their wounds.

Pity kills

And digs the graves

For Living Dead

Who, lying buried

Under piles of vain excuses,

Mock creation's purpose.

STREPHONADE

Should love become despair

And should I never touch

Your hand again,

I'll feel it there.

Just like the thread

Unseverable

We wound

Around us

Bound

So when I die

I'll feel the pull and pain

Until we touch again.

36

YOU DO NOT COMMAND

You do not command

Nor exact of me a price,

Nor look on me

And wish adjustment

Of the image

To your clarity,

Or twist my thoughts

To bend with yours,

No . . .

There's air to breathe,

A growing room,

A galaxy of space

Set with your sun.

I turn to your rhythm!

Master?

Yes,

He who commands not!

37

TWO IN ONE

Sometimes we are one

But most times two

Solitudes,

Like gulls flying

In tandem

Or dancers

Touching lightly

Moving

To the same rhythm.

As we talk here

On the sand

Our coalescence

Compounds

To magnitudes

Far beyond

The castles

We would build

Alone.

WHAT'S THE SCORE?

Aristotle said

Women have less

teeth than men.

No one doubted

'til one day when

someone thought

to count

and found

both had

the same amount.

39

THE NEED

(from E. Fromm)

From birth cut off

With one quick clip,

We quest our lives away

To link with

Some Great Joy

Who joins us with

Humanity again.

We wail at that

First separation

And later cry, too, at the

Tender friction of

Two souls coinciding,

Certain together

We will make Heaven again.

40

INTERIM

How far away

Is time and space

This capsulation hour

From world or place,

The only life, the only touch,

The only conscious form —

The warp and woof of us.

Yet we celebrate love

With all we touch and see

As *the* most real

Of all reality.

41

SYNAPSE

The world was just a carousel

Of tarnished horses,

Peeling paint,

Music winding

Down

A

Half-

Tone

Low,

Then

You came to show

Colors I had never found,

Larks tearing up the air with sound,

Laughter seeming to weep for joy

Because containing was too much

When in this wild-spun world we touched!

42

THE QUARREL

You left me feeling

like a moldy orange peel

run over by a garbage truck

left in the gutter

to biodegrade.

Long ago

when I was still

on the Yellow Brick Road to Oz

I turned the orange

inside out

to get it all.

I just did that again

And you ate it to the white.

That made it easier to smash.

43

ON SEEING AN OLD BOYFRIEND

Am I fatter?

What does it matter.

We're both married,

No need to flatter.

Losing your hair?

I really don't care

How many kids?

Now let's compare.

Same old grin,

Where have you been?

Give a hundred dollars

If I looked thin.

44

HOW MANY BEAUTIES MISSED

Just one zip
Of your wings
Past my table
And you would be a patch
On my swatter,
Fly on my curtain.
I've never bothered
To watch you
At leisure,
Painted Cadillacblack,
Iridescent in royal blue
Body suit, trimmed
Delicately with veined
Transparencies of wings.
You're beautiful . . .
    But that's the end
    Of our conversation.
    I almost forgot
    Your bad reputation!

45

HUMOR BONES

Everyone needs

a funky aunt

who rides merry-go-rounds

at family reunions

and spits watermelon seeds

at kids.

The rest lump up

in arthritic groups,

looking as if

life's bleak intensity

had bleached their

humor bones.

    Then she softens all the grim

       By singing Please Don't Fence Me In

       As if it were a hymn.

"WHERE THERE IS NO VISION . . ."

Remembering
is a kind of pain,
dredging up
those ragged memories,
faded as a prom corsage
pressed flat,
as out-of-date
as penny loafers
or the Hit Parade.

For me, serve up
dew-spangled
New Day,
untouched,
malleable,
liquid.
I love The Now,

But not as well
as The Tomorrows,
for moments stay
just long enough
to leave and
dreams and hopes
are better far
than memories.

47

SINGING IN A CAPPELLA CHOIR

All

I hear

is the voice

of us, one throat,

one body, am I singing

at all, singing at all, being

meshed in corporate electricity,

leaning forward, lifting, rising, soaring

S'ma Yisroel, HALLELUJAH, HALLELUJAH, Elohenu,

as torrents in summer, praise Him, gather

like fabric on a thread, smooth now

for He hath given His angels

a charge concerning you,

walk barefoot on a

cloud softly

pianissimo

Amen.

BETROTHAL

I fear for my own joy

And start at my own shadow

Next to yours.

The glare of you

Splits up reality

Into raw splinters

Of a dream

I never dared before.

Eternity

Will not be long enough.

49

WEDDING NIGHT

I love you with the ease

Of sun warming the day,

Innately, as a bird

Feeding her young,

As surely as the bee

Is drawn among

The vines of honeysuckle there —

But yet with tidal power!

How much we dare

In this sweet counting hour,

Releasing free the lock

That stays the flow!

Take! Take!

Of my unending store,

I can contain no more!

TRILOGY

I

I wonder if in Heaven
I shouted when you were born,
Knowing someday the joy
Of Us would happen,
And the creation of me
Would never be complete
Until this fusion
And together we'd find why
God really made the world!

II

Who said you fall in love
As if it were an accident
Or trap?
We walked in love,
Sometimes ran,
'Til now
We stand in love
Fathoms deep,
Oceans wide!

III

If when I die
You bend in sorrow
By a withered me,
I shall be young again,
The beauty of our nows
Will hang about,
My spirit will reach out
To touch you
Just once more,
So waiting will be bearable
Until you come.

ETERNAL LIVES

I in you

You in me,

Limitless the

Powers that be.

From Heaven to earth

From sun to star,

Eternity

Is what we are.

52

MARRIAGE IS ALIVE AND WELL

Peace is in your touch,

a balm immersing,

quenching tiny fires,

smoothing day's jagged edges,

wanding away world noise,

as soft as healing,

a soul-bent missile

53

bringing your strength

with power left

to jettison a twinge

straight to my heart

enough to make shouting of love

a wish to take away the pain.

SKYBIRD

Turkeys and chickens

never get far off the ground

      and usually they're found

on plates, ending up

de-fleshed in garbage cans.

But skybirds

54

see the world,

slice through clouds,

conversing with the sun,

far above the barnyard dung,

      star hung

they are.

   O let me

      be a skybird!

DANCE AT MY DEATH

Dance at my death?
Of course,
For I am that much closer
To the stars,
Or play
Or sing —
Most anything
But weep.

I would not like
To lie beneath
Intemperate amounts
Of ill-afforded flowers
Or see my friends
Dark-robed and sad
Instead of glad.

I go with joy!
So dress in rainbows
On that day,
Play the music
Loud and gay,
Dance 'til you
Are out of breath,
Make joy and beauty
Of my death!

55

I LOVE TO DRAW DRAPES ON THE WORLD

I love to draw drapes on the world
To watch my mind's wild circus.

Clown words
Bump,
Burst,
Disappear,
Diverge,
Converge,
Then adhere,
Railroad off cliffs
And sentence edges,
Chug down blind alleys,
And sticky hedges,
Snowballing
Into paragraphs,
Settling down
In well-worn paths,
After a brief
Vacuous drought,
Widen to
Silent valleys of thought.

AUTOMATION

Lucifer planned efficiently,

Programming to conduct

A way whereby we lose control

And quickly self-destruct.

AGAPE

I am so deep in loving,

There is no concern

In asking whether or not

You love me in return.

PARTING

Stay, O stay, sweet morning!
Though your bright hours break and run,
And the morning glory folds away
With the passing of the sun!

58

The night moves close around me
Like an eyeless shroud of sorrow.
O promise me before you leave
The sun will rise tomorrow!